Our Favorite
Flavors of
the Seasons

Try serving "light" dippers with hearty full-flavored dips and spreads.
Bite-size baby vegetables, pita wedges, baked tortilla chips and
multi-grain crispbread are all sturdy enough to scoop,
yet won't overshadow the flavor of the dip.

Roasted Red Pepper & Artichoke Dip

8-oz. pkg. cream cheese, softened
8-oz. container sour cream
1 c. shredded mozzarella cheese
1/2 c. grated Parmesan cheese
13-oz. jar marinated artichoke
    hearts, drained and quartered

12-oz. jar roasted red peppers,
    drained and chopped
1/2 c. banana peppers, chopped
5 cloves garlic, chopped
toasted baguette slices

Melt cream cheese in a large skillet over low heat, stirring until smooth. Remove from heat. Stir in sour cream, mozzarella cheese and Parmesan cheese, blending well. Return to medium-low heat. Stir in remaining ingredients except baguettes; heat through. Serve warm with toasted baguette slices.

Autumn can be so busy! If time is tight, streamline your holiday plans...just ask your family what traditions and festive foods they cherish the most. Then focus on tried & true activities and free up time to try something new..

Cheddar-Sausage Cornbread Balls

Makes one to 1-1/2 dozen

15-oz. pkg. cornbread mix
1 lb. ground pork sausage

3 c. shredded Cheddar cheese
1 c. half-and-half

Add cornbread mix to a large bowl. Break up sausage into small pieces over cornbread mix. Add cheese and toss together with your hands, working cornbread mix into the sausage. Pour half-and-half over all; mix together with your hands. Shape into 2-inch balls; arrange on a parchment paper-lined baking sheet. Bake at 375 degrees for 15 to 20 minutes, until golden. To check for doneness, cut one ball in half. Sausage should be browned, while bread will look moist and solid, yet tender.

Back-to-school time isn't just for kids. Treat yourself to a class that you've been longing to try...whether it's knitting, cooking, yoga or even a foreign language. Take along a friend for twice the fun!

Cranberry-Orange Snack Mix

Makes 11 cups

3 c. bite-size crispy corn
   cereal squares
3 c. bite-size crispy rice
   cereal squares
3 c. bite-size crispy wheat
   cereal squares
1 c. sliced almonds or other nuts

1 c. pretzel rings or sticks
1/4 c. butter, sliced
1/4 c. brown sugar, packed
1/4 c. frozen orange juice
   concentrate, thawed
1 c. dried cranberries
1 c. white chocolate chips

In a large bowl, mix cereals, nuts and pretzels; set aside. In a microwave-safe bowl, combine butter, brown sugar and orange juice. Microwave on high for 20 seconds; stir. Pour over cereal mixture; stir until evenly coated. Pour cereal mixture into a lightly greased large roasting pan. Bake, uncovered, at 300 degrees for 30 minutes, stirring after 15 minutes. Remove from oven; cool completely. Stir in cranberries and chocolate chips. Store in an airtight container.

How spooky...mummy dogs! Simply wrap strips of bread stick dough around hot dogs. Arrange them on an ungreased baking sheet and bake at 375 degrees for 12 to 15 minutes, until golden. Add eyes with dots of catsup or mustard.

Upside-Down Pizza

Serves 6 to 8

1 lb. ground Italian mild
   pork sausage
3/4 c. onion, chopped
15-1/2 oz. jar pizza sauce
4-oz. sliced black olives, drained
4-oz. can sliced mushrooms,
   drained
2 to 3 c. shredded mozzarella
   cheese

2 eggs, beaten
1 c. milk
1 T. oil
1 c. all-purpose flour
1/4 t. salt
1/4 c. grated Parmesan cheese

In a skillet over medium heat, brown sausage with onion; drain. Add pizza sauce, olives and mushrooms; cook until bubbly and spoon into a greased 13"x9" baking pan. Spread mozzarella cheese evenly over top. Combine eggs, milk, oil, flour and salt in a blender; process until smooth (or stir together in a bowl). Pour batter over mozzarella cheese; sprinkle with Parmesan cheese. Bake, uncovered, at 400 degrees for about 30 minutes, until puffed and golden. Cut into squares and serve immediately.

Invite friends and neighbors over for a backyard festival on a sunny autumn day. Games like cornhole, bobbing for apples, Red Rover and three-legged races add old-fashioned fun!

Zucchini & Sausage Casserole

Serves 8 to 10

1 lb. ground sweet Italian pork
    sausage, browned and drained
8-1/2 oz. pkg. cornbread mix
10-oz. pkg. frozen corn, thawed
3 c. zucchini, shredded
1 onion, finely chopped

2 eggs, beaten
1-1/2 t. garlic, minced
1/2 t. dried dill weed
1/2 t. salt
1-1/4 c. shredded Cheddar
    cheese, divided

Combine sausage and dry cornbread mix in a lightly greased 2-quart casserole dish. Add remaining ingredients, setting aside 1/4 cup cheese for topping. Mix gently. Bake, uncovered, at 350 degrees for about 50 minutes, until a knife tip inserted in the center comes out clean. Top with reserved cheese; return to oven long enough to melt the cheese.

Thanksgiving dinner is all about tradition! Keep it simple with tried & true recipes everyone loves and looks for...sweet potato casserole, corn pudding and cranberry sauce. Perhaps add just one or two simple new dishes for variety. Then relax and enjoy your guests!

Herbed Turkey Breast

4 to 5-lb. turkey breast, thawed
   if frozen
6 T. butter, softened
1 T. fresh parsley, finely chopped
1 T. fresh sage, finely chopped

1 T. fresh thyme, finely chopped
2 t. salt
1/2 t. pepper
1 c. chicken broth

Pat turkey breast dry with paper towels. Gently separate the skin, leaving it attached around the edges. Blend butter, herbs and seasonings in a small bowl; rub butter mixture underneath skin. Place breast in an ungreased shallow roasting pan. Bake, uncovered, at 325 degrees for one hour and 45 minutes to 2 hours, basting several times while baking, until a meat thermometer inserted in thickest part reads 165 degrees. Remove breast to a deep platter; lightly tent with aluminum foil and let stand for 15 minutes. Meanwhile, add chicken broth to juices in roasting pan; scrape up browned bits in the bottom of pan and transfer to a saucepan. Let stand a few minutes; spoon off fat. Bring broth mixture to a boil over high heat; boil until cooked down to 3/4 cup. Slice turkey thinly; ladle broth mixture over turkey.

Greet your guests with a whimsical pumpkin tower on the front porch. Arrange pumpkins and squash in graduated sizes in a stack, using skewers to hold them in place. Clever!.

Turkey Enchilada Skillet

2 T. olive oil
1/2 c. onion, chopped
1/2 c. red pepper, chopped
2 cloves garlic, chopped
2 16-oz. jars red or green salsa
15-1/2 oz. can black beans,
    drained and rinsed

8-3/4 oz. can corn, drained
2 c. cooked turkey or
    chicken, cubed
2 c. cooked rice
salt and pepper to taste
1 to 2 c. shredded Mexican-blend
    cheese

Heat oil in a large skillet over medium heat; add onion, red pepper and garlic. Cook for 2 to 3 minutes, stirring occasionally, until onion is nearly tender. Stir in salsa, beans, corn, turkey or chicken and rice. Simmer for 6 to 8 minutes, stirring occasionally. Season with salt and pepper. Remove from heat; sprinkle with cheese. Cover and let stand for several minutes, until cheese is melted.

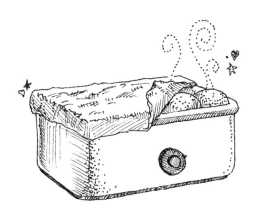

Warm sandwich buns for a crowd...easy! Fill a roaster with buns, cover with heavy-duty aluminum foil and cut several slits in the foil. Top with several dampened paper towels and tightly cover with more foil. Bake at 250 degrees for 20 minutes. Rolls will be hot and steamy.

Bake-All-Day Barbecue Beef

Serves 12

5 to 6-lb. beef chuck roast
1 c. onion, finely chopped
1 clove garlic, minced
4 c. ginger ale
3 c. catsup
2 T. Worcestershire sauce

1 T. white vinegar
1 t. salt
1/2 t. pepper
1/2 t. dry mustard
1/8 t. lemon juice
12 hamburger buns, split

Place roast in a large Dutch oven. In a large bowl, whisk together remaining ingredients except buns; spoon over roast. Cover and bake at 300 degrees for 6 to 8 hours, until roast is tender. May also be cooked in a slow cooker on low setting for 9 to 11 hours. Shred roast with 2 forks; serve beef on buns.

An open home, an open heart,
here grows a bountiful harvest.

–Judy Hand

Butterball Biscuits

Makes one dozen

1/2 c. butter, melted and divided
2 c. all-purpose flour
1 T. baking powder
1 t. salt
1/3 c. butter, softened
3/4 c. milk

Spoon one teaspoon melted butter into each of 12 muffin cups; set aside remaining melted butter. In a large bowl, sift together flour, baking powder and salt. Add softened butter; cut in with a pastry blender until mixture resembles cornmeal. Stir in milk with a fork. Fill each muffin cup nearly to the top with batter. Bake at 450 degrees for 10 minutes. Spoon one teaspoon remaining melted butter over each biscuit; bake for 10 minutes more.

Apple picking can be a fun family outing! The kids will be amazed to see all the different kinds of apples and so many are just the right size for little ones. Take a picnic and make a day of it, with fresh-picked apples for dessert!

Pumpkin Pie Applesauce

6 apples, peeled, cored and diced
2/3 c. apple cider or juice
2/3 c. canned pumpkin
1/4 c. brown sugar, packed,
   or to taste

2 t. pumpkin pie spice
1/4 t. cinnamon

Combine all ingredients in a large saucepan; bring to a low boil over
medium heat. Reduce heat to medium-low and simmer for about
30 minutes, until apples are very soft and tender. Using a potato masher,
an electric mixer or an immersion blender, purée applesauce mixture to
desired consistency. Serve warm or chilled.

For an autumn centerpiece that only takes a moment, place a pumpkin on a cake stand and tuck some bittersweet sprigs around it. Simple yet so eye-catching.

Best Cheesy Potatoes

Makes 10 to 12 servings

30-oz. pkg. frozen diced
　　hashbrown potatoes
10-3/4 oz. can cream of
　　chicken soup
1 to 2 8-oz. pkgs. shredded
　　Cheddar cheese
16-oz. container sour cream

2 t. sweet onion, chopped
1 t. salt
1/4 t. pepper
2 c. corn flake cereal, crushed
1/4 c. butter, melted

In a large bowl, combine all ingredients except cereal and butter; stir well.
Spread in a lightly greased 13"x9" baking pan. Combine crushed corn
flakes and melted butter; top potatoes with mixture. Bake, uncovered,
at 350 degrees for one hour, or until bubbly and golden.

Fruity gelatin salads are yummy topped with a dollop of creamy lemon mayonnaise. Combine 1/2 cup mayonnaise and 3 tablespoons each of lemon juice, light cream and powdered sugar. Garnish with a sprinkle of lemon zest, if desired.

Cranberry Pretzel Salad

Serves 12

2 c. boiling water
6-oz. pkg. black cherry gelatin mix
2 15-oz. cans whole-berry
   cranberry sauce
2 c. pretzel twists, finely crushed

3/4 c. butter, melted
1/2 c. plus 1 T. sugar, divided
8-oz. pkg. cream cheese, softened
8-oz. container frozen whipped
   topping, thawed

In a bowl, stir together boiling water and gelatin mix for 2 minutes, or until dissolved. Stir in cranberry sauce. Cover and refrigerate until cooled and partially set. Meanwhile, in a separate bowl, mix together crushed pretzels, melted butter and one tablespoon sugar. Press into the bottom of an ungreased 13"x9" glass baking pan. Bake at 350 degrees for 8 minutes; set aside to cool. In another bowl, blend together cream cheese, whipped topping and remaining sugar; spread over cooled crust. Spoon cooled gelatin over cream cheese mixture. Cover and refrigerate overnight, or until set. Cut into squares.

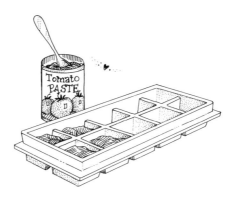

A spoonful or two of tomato paste adds rich flavor to soups and
stews. If you have a partial can left over, freeze the rest in
ice cube trays, then pop out and store in a freezer bag.
Frozen cubes can be dropped right into simmering
dishes...no need to thaw.

Farmstand Vegetable Soup

Makes 8 servings

2 T. olive oil
2 c. onions, thinly sliced
1 c. celery, thinly sliced
2 t. Italian seasoning
salt and pepper to taste
3 14-1/2 oz. cans chicken broth
28-oz. can petite diced tomatoes

1 T. tomato paste
3 c. water
8 c. chopped or sliced vegetables
like potatoes, carrots, corn,
green beans, lima beans
and peas

Heat oil in a large stockpot over medium heat. Add onions, celery and Italian seasoning; season with salt and pepper. Cook, stirring often, until onions are translucent, 5 to 8 minutes. Add chicken broth, tomatoes with juice, tomato paste and 3 cups water to pot; stir well and bring to a boil. Reduce heat to medium-low. Simmer, uncovered, for 20 minutes. Add vegetables to pot; return to a simmer. Cook, uncovered, until vegetables are tender, 20 to 25 minutes.

Take an autumn bike ride...fill the bike's basket
with a thermos of soup and a loaf of bread.
What fun!

October Bisque

Makes 8 servings

1 onion, chopped
1/4 c. butter
4 c. chicken broth
28-oz. can whole tomatoes

1 T. sugar
2 15-oz. cans pumpkin
2 T. fresh parsley, chopped
2 T. fresh chives, chopped

Sauté onion in butter until onion is tender. Add broth and simmer for 15 minutes. Add tomatoes with juice to a blender or food processor and blend until smooth. Add tomato mixture, sugar, pumpkin, parsley and chives to broth; heat through.

"Dirt" cupcakes are such fun for kids! Bake up chocolate cupcakes using your favorite recipe. When cool, top them with chocolate frosting and sprinkle with crushed chocolate sandwich cookie "dirt." Decorate with colorful gummy worms...eek!

Caramel Apple Cupcakes

Makes 2 dozen

18-1/4 oz. pkg. spice cake mix
2 McIntosh apples, peeled, cored
    and diced
14-oz. pkg. caramels, unwrapped

3 T. milk
Optional: chopped walnuts
    or pecans

Prepare cake mix as package directs; fold apples into batter. Spoon batter into 24 greased or paper-lined muffin cups, filling 2/3 full. Bake at 350 degrees for 20 to 25 minutes. Cool cupcakes on a wire rack. Combine caramels and milk in a saucepan over medium heat. Cook, stirring constantly, until completely melted; spread over cupcakes. Sprinkle with nuts, if desired.

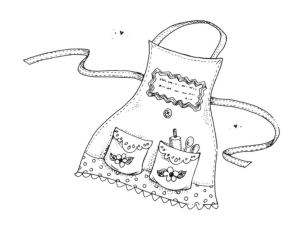

Little ones love to help out in the kitchen, so tuck a set of
measuring spoons, oven mitt and mini rolling pin in the pocket
of a child-size apron...everything a little helper needs.

Warm Banana Bread Cobbler

1-1/2 c. self-rising flour, divided
1 c. sugar
3/4 c. milk
1/2 c. butter, melted
1 t. vanilla extract
4 ripe bananas, sliced

1 c. rolled oats, uncooked
3/4 c. brown sugar, packed
1/2 c. butter, softened
1/2 c. chopped walnuts
Garnish: vanilla ice cream

In a bowl, stir together one cup flour and sugar. Add milk, melted butter and vanilla; stir until smooth. Spread batter evenly in a buttered rectangular 3-quart casserole dish. Top with sliced bananas; set aside. In a separate large bowl, combine oats, brown sugar and remaining flour. With a pastry cutter, cut in softened butter until crumbly; stir in walnuts. Sprinkle mixture over bananas. Bake at 375 degrees for 25 to 30 minutes, until set and golden. Serve warm, topped with ice cream.

Serve up a Bucket o' Bones at your next Halloween party!
Press a mini marshmallow onto each end of a pretzel stick
and dip in melted white chocolate.

Spiderweb Cookies

16-1/2 oz. tube refrigerated
    sugar cookie dough
3 c. powdered sugar
3 T. light corn syrup

1/2 t. vanilla extract
3 T. plus 3 t. milk, divided
2 T. baking cocoa

Slice dough into 16 rounds. Place 2 inches apart on ungreased baking sheets. Bake at 350 degrees for 12 to 14 minutes. Transfer to a wire rack to cool. Blend powdered sugar, corn syrup, vanilla and 3 tablespoons plus one teaspoon milk until smooth. Measure 1/3 cup of frosting mixture into a small bowl; stir in cocoa and remaining milk. Transfer chocolate frosting to a plastic zipping bag; snip off corner. Turn cookies so flat sides are up. Working on one cookie at a time, spread white frosting over top. Beginning in the center, pipe on a spiral of chocolate frosting. Starting in center of spiral, pull a knife tip through the spiral to create a spiderweb pattern.

Make a party tray of savory bite-size appetizer tarts...
guests will never suspect how easy it is! Bake frozen mini
phyllo shells according to package directions. Cool,
then spoon in a favorite creamy dip or spread.

Bacon-Wrapped Water Chestnuts

2 8-oz. cans water chestnuts,
    drained
1 lb. bacon, each slice cut into
    3 pieces

1/2 c. brown sugar, packed
1/2 c. catsup

Wrap each water chestnut in a piece of bacon; fasten with a wooden
toothpick. Arrange on a baking sheet coated with non-stick vegetable
spray. Bake at 400 degrees for 45 minutes to one hour, until bacon is crisp.
Combine brown sugar and catsup in a bowl; spoon over chestnuts. Reduce
oven to 350 degrees; bake for an additional 30 to 45 minutes, until glazed.

At Christmas, when old friends are meeting,
We give that long-loved joyous greeting...
Merry Christmas!

–Dorothy Brown Thompson

Linda's Holiday Cranberry Salsa *Makes 10 to 12 servings*

12-oz. pkg. cranberries,
    thawed if frozen
1 c. sugar
6 green onions, chopped
1/2 c. fresh cilantro, chopped

1 jalapeño pepper, seeded and
    finely chopped
8-oz. pkg. cream cheese, softened
assorted crackers or tortilla chips

Combine cranberries and sugar in a food processor; pulse until coarsely chopped. Transfer to a bowl; add onions, cilantro and jalapeño pepper. Mix well. Cover and refrigerate several hours or overnight. To serve, unwrap cream cheese and place on a serving plate. Drain salsa; spoon over cream cheese. Serve with crackers or tortilla chips.

Make your own tasty pita chips. Split 3 pita rounds and cut each
into 8 wedges. Brush with 3 tablespoons olive oil on both sides;
sprinkle with salt and pepper. Arrange in a single layer on
a lightly greased baking sheet. Bake at 375 degrees for
6 minutes on each side, until crisp.

Traditional Christmas Hot Crab Dip

Serves 15

1-1/4 c. butter
7 T. green onions, sliced
7 T. all-purpose flour
1-1/4 t. salt
1/8 t. cayenne pepper

2-1/4 c. half-and-half
3-1/2 c. shredded Swiss cheese
1 lb. white crabmeat, flaked
1/8 t. hot pepper sauce
corn chips or crackers

Melt butter in a large skillet over medium heat; sauté onions. Add flour, salt and pepper; stir until smooth. Remove from heat; slowly pour in half-and-half, stirring constantly. Return to low heat. Add cheese; stir until melted. Fold in crabmeat; season with hot pepper sauce. Keep warm in a chafing dish or small slow cooker set on warm. Serve with corn chips or crackers.

Share the stories behind the special foods that are a tradition
at your family's holiday dinners...Grandmother's baked beans,
Aunt Jessie's famous walnut cake, Mom's secret seasoning for
the roast beef. There may even be stories to tell about the
vintage tablecloth or the whimsical salt & pepper shakers!

Elegant Beef & Noodles

3 lbs. beef sirloin, cut into cubes
10-1/2 oz. can French onion soup
10-1/2 oz. can beef consommé
1 c. vegetable cocktail juice
1 c. Burgundy wine or beef broth
1/2 c. brown sugar, packed
1 t. garlic powder

1 t. dried oregano
1/2 t. celery salt
2 bay leaves
3 T. cornstarch
1/3 c. cold water
2 to 3 c. egg noodles, cooked
butter to taste

Place beef cubes in a Dutch oven. Add soups, vegetable juice, wine or broth, brown sugar and seasonings; mix gently. Cover and bake at 300 degrees for 3 to 4 hours, stirring occasionally. Remove from oven; discard bay leaves. Combine cornstarch and cold water in a small bowl, stirring well. Stir cornstarch mixture into beef mixture. Place Dutch oven on stovetop; cook and stir over medium-high heat until gravy thickens. Toss noodles with butter; serve beef and gravy over noodles.

For old-fashioned farmhouse charm, group together an assortment
of vintage tin graters on a tabletop or mantel. Tuck a tea light
under each and enjoy their cozy flickering lights.

One-Pot Pork Chop Dinner

Makes 6 servings

6 pork chops, 3/4-inch thick
1 T. oil
1 onion, sliced
1 green pepper, chopped
4-oz. can mushroom stems &
    pieces, drained

8-oz. can tomato sauce
1 T. brown sugar, packed
2 t. Worcestershire sauce
1-1/2 t. cider vinegar
1/2 t. salt
cooked rice

In a skillet over medium heat, brown pork chops in oil on both sides; drain. Transfer pork chops to a 6-quart slow cooker; add onion, green pepper and mushrooms. In a bowl, combine remaining ingredients except rice. Spoon over pork chops and vegetables. Cover and cook on low setting for 4 to 5 hours, until pork chops are tender. Serve over cooked rice.

Share the joy! Call a local college and invite an out-of-town student
to dinner who won't be going home over the long holidays.
Or perhaps your church can suggest an older person who is
on her own. The more, the merrier!

Baked Macaroni My Way

Makes 6 servings

8-oz. pkg. elbow macaroni, uncooked
3 c. chicken broth
4 T. butter, sliced and divided
1/2 c. green pepper, chopped
1/4 c. sweet onion, chopped
1/4 c. celery, finely chopped
1/2 c. sliced mushrooms
1/2 c. sliced green olives with pimentos
1-1/2 c. cooked ham, cubed
1 c. shredded sharp Cheddar cheese
10-3/4 oz. can tomato soup
3 slices bacon

Cook macaroni in broth with one tablespoon butter, according to package directions; drain. Meanwhile, sauté green pepper, onion and celery in remaining butter for about 5 minutes, until soft. Combine cooked macaroni, pepper mixture and remaining ingredients except bacon. Mix well; transfer to a greased 2-quart casserole dish. Arrange bacon slices on top. Bake, uncovered, at 400 degrees for 20 minutes, or until bubbly and bacon is crisp.

On Christmas, younger family members may be too busy playing with new toys to enjoy a sit-down dinner. Instead, set out a buffet of sliced ham, baked beans, potato salad, fruit salad, rolls and bread, and a platter of Christmas cookies for dessert. Everyone can "graze" as they like.

Scalloped Potatoes & Ham

Serves 6

2 T. onion, chopped
1/4 c. butter
1/4 c. all-purpose flour
1/2 t. dry mustard
1 t. salt
1/8 t. pepper

1-1/2 c. milk
2 c. shredded Cheddar cheese,
  divided
6 c. potatoes, peeled, cooked
  and sliced
1-1/2 c. cooked ham, cubed

In a skillet over medium heat, sauté onion in butter. Blend in flour, mustard, salt and pepper. Gradually add milk, stirring constantly until thickened. Mix in 1-1/2 cups cheese and stir until melted. Remove from heat; add potatoes and toss to coat. Spoon mixture into a greased 13"x9" baking pan. Arrange ham on top; sprinkle with remaining cheese. Bake, uncovered, at 350 degrees for 30 minutes, or until hot and bubbly.

Keep a crock of herbed garlic butter in the fridge for
jazzing up steamed veggies or making garlic bread. Simply
blend one teaspoon each of Italian seasoning, dried mustard
and garlic powder into 1/2 cup softened butter. Mmm good!

Shrimp Fettuccine Alfredo

16-oz. pkg. fettuccine pasta, uncooked

3/4 c. half-and-half

3/4 c. grated Pecorino Romano cheese, divided

1/2 lb. uncooked large shrimp, peeled and cleaned

1/2 c. butter, melted

Cook pasta according to package directions; drain. Meanwhile, in a large bowl, mix together half-and-half and half of grated cheese. Add cooked pasta; toss to coat and set aside. Add shrimp to a saucepan of boiling water. Boil for 3 to 4 minutes, just until pink. Drain; add melted butter to shrimp and toss to coat. Add shrimp mixture to pasta mixture and toss well. Top with remaining cheese and serve.

Keep rolls warm at dinner. Before arranging rolls in
a bread basket, place a terra-cotta warming tile in the
bottom and line with a Christmasy tea towel.

Crazy-Good Popovers

Makes about one dozen

2 c. biscuit baking mix
2/3 c. milk
1/2 c. shredded Cheddar cheese
4 green onions, chopped

8 slices bacon, crisply cooked
   and crumbled
2 T. butter, melted

In a large bowl, combine all ingredients except butter. Mix thoroughly until a soft dough forms. Drop dough by tablespoonfuls onto a baking sheet sprayed with non-stick vegetable spray. Bake at 450 degrees for 7 to 9 minutes, until golden. Brush with melted butter; serve warm.

As Christmas nears, plan a family slumber party! Set up
quilts and sleeping bags around the tree, pass around lots of
snacks and watch a holiday movie. Before falling asleep,
read "*The Night Before Christmas*" with only
the tree lights on.

Winter Garden Salad

1 head cauliflower, cut into
 bite-size pieces
1 bunch broccoli, cut into
 bite-size pieces
1/2 c. onion, chopped
1/4 c. green onions, chopped

1/4 c. celery, chopped
1/2 c. carrot, peeled and chopped
1 c. Cheddar cheese, diced
1/4 c. bacon, crisply cooked and
 crumbled

Combine all ingredients in a salad bowl; toss to mix. Pour Dressing over all; toss again. Cover and refrigerate for 8 to 10 hours. Toss again just before serving. Makes 8 servings.

Dressing:

1/2 c. mayonnaise
1/3 c. vinegar

1/3 c. oil
1/3 c. sugar

Combine all ingredients in a jar; add lid and shake well.

Place newly arrived Christmas cards in a vintage napkin holder,
then take a moment every evening to share happy holiday
greetings from friends & neighbors over dinner!

Sweet Potato Crisp

Serves 10 to 12

4-1/2 c. sweet potatoes, peeled,
    cubed, cooked and mashed
3/4 c. sugar
3/8 c. milk

1/2 c. butter, melted
1-1/2 t. vanilla extract
2 eggs, beaten

In a large saucepan, cover sweet potatoes with water; bring to a boil over high heat. Cook until fork-tender; drain. Add potatoes to a large bowl; mash well. Add remaining ingredients; mix well. Spoon potato mixture into a greased 2-quart casserole dish. Spoon Topping over casserole. Bake, uncovered, at 375 degrees for about 30 minutes, until crisp and golden.

Topping:

1-1/2 c. all-purpose flour
3/4 c. sugar
3/4 c. light brown sugar, packed

1 c. old-fashioned oats, uncooked
1/2 t. salt
1 c. chilled butter, diced

In a large bowl, mix all ingredients except butter. Add butter; beat with an electric mixer on medium speed until well mixed.

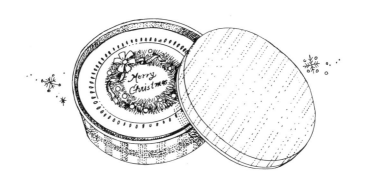

Don't save them for "someday," make some memories now...
go ahead and use Grandma's best china and silver!

Mom's Cheesy Broccoli Bake

Makes 6 servings

10-oz. frozen chopped broccoli
10-3/4 oz. can cream of
　　mushroom soup
1/2 c. shredded Cheddar cheese
1 egg, beaten

1/4 c. mayonnaise
1/4 c. milk
1 T. butter, melted
1/4 c. dry bread crumbs

Cook broccoli according to package directions; drain well. Meanwhile, in a large bowl, blend mushroom soup, cheese and egg; stir in mayonnaise and milk. Fold in broccoli; transfer to a lightly greased 10"x6" baking pan. In a small bowl, mix melted butter and bread crumbs; sprinkle on top. Bake, uncovered, at 375 degrees for 30 to 35 minutes, until bubbly and crumbs are golden.

Thank God for dirty dishes,
They have a tale to tell.
While others may go hungry,
We're eating very well.

– Author Unknown

Easy Italian Wedding Soup

Serves 4

2 14-1/2 oz. cans chicken broth
1 c. water
1 c. medium shell pasta, uncooked

16 frozen meatballs, cooked
2 c. fresh spinach, finely shredded
1 c. pizza sauce

Bring broth and one cup water to a boil in a large saucepan over medium-high heat; add pasta and meatballs. Return to a boil; cook for 7 to 9 minutes, until pasta is tender. Do not drain. Reduce heat; stir in spinach and pizza sauce. Cook for one to 2 minutes, until heated through.

Heap on the wood! the wind is chill;
But let it whistle as it will,
We'll keep our Christmas merry still!

–Sir Walter Scott

Snowy-Day Stew

3 T. oil
2 lbs. stew beef cubes
1 clove garlic, minced
4 cubes beef bouillon
4 c. boiling water
1 t. dried rosemary
1 t. dried parsley
1/2 t. pepper
3 russet potatoes, peeled and cubed

4 carrots, peeled and cut into
  1-inch pieces
4 stalks celery, cut into 1-inch
  pieces
1 c. onion, chopped
1 c. frozen green peas
5 t. cornstarch
2 t. cold water

Heat oil in a large skillet over medium heat. Add beef cubes and garlic; brown well on all sides. Add bouillon cubes to boiling water; let stand until dissolved. Transfer beef mixture to a 6-quart slow cooker. Add bouillon mixture and remaining ingredients except cornstarch and cold water; stir well. Cover and cook on high setting for 4 hours, or on low setting for 8 hours, until beef and vegetables are tender. Dissolve cornstarch in cold water; stir into stew. Cover and cook on high setting for an additional 30 minutes to thicken.

Make a neighborly gesture! Deliver a small decorated tree
and a plate of cookies to an acquaintance who can't go
out easily. Even better, send the kids to do it.

Strawberries in the Snow

Serves 8 to 10

16-oz. container strawberries,
  hulled and sliced
sugar to taste
8-oz. pkg. cream cheese, softened
14-oz. can sweetened
  condensed milk

1 bakery sour cream angel food
  cake, sliced or torn into pieces
  and divided
8-oz. container frozen whipped
  topping, thawed

In a bowl, combine strawberries and sugar to taste; toss to mix and set
aside. In a large bowl, beat cream cheese and condensed milk with an
electric mixer on medium speed until smooth. In a clear glass bowl, layer
1/3 each of cake, cream cheese mixture and strawberries. Repeat layers
twice; spread with whipped topping. Cover and refrigerate until chilled.

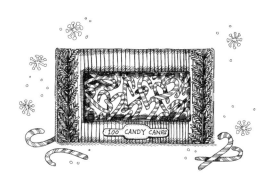

100 CANDY CANES

To easily crush candy canes for holiday garnishes, place candy in a plastic zipping bag and tap gently with a wooden mallet or rolling pin.

Christmas Peppermint Cookies

Makes 1-1/2 dozen

1/2 c. butter, softened
1/4 c. oil
1 egg, beaten
1/2 c. powdered sugar
1/2 c. sugar

1/2 t. baking soda
1/2 t. salt
1/2 t. cream of tartar
2 c. all-purpose flour
2 t. vanilla extract

Combine all ingredients in a large bowl; mix well. Cover and chill until firm. Drop dough onto ungreased baking sheets, 3 level tablespoons per cookie. Bake at 350 degrees for 10 to 12 minutes, until golden. Remove cookies to wire racks; cool. Spread Icing over cookies.

Icing:

1/4 c. butter, melted
1/8 t. salt
2 c. powdered sugar

1 drop red food coloring
1/4 c. peppermint candies, crushed

Combine butter, salt and powdered sugar; mix well. Stir in food coloring; fold in crushed candies.

Be sure to pick up a pint or two of ice cream in cinnamon, peppermint and other delicious seasonal flavors when they're available. What a special touch for holiday desserts!

Grandma's Gingerbread Cake

Serves 12 to 15

3 c. all-purpose flour
1 t. baking soda
1 t. ground ginger
1 t. ground cloves
1 t. cinnamon

1 c. brown sugar, packed
1/2 c. margarine, melted
1 c. molasses
2 eggs
1 c. boiling water

In a large bowl, sift together flour, baking soda and spices; set aside. In another bowl, stir brown sugar into melted margarine. Add molasses and unbeaten eggs; beat well. Add flour mixture and boiling water to brown sugar mixture alternately in small amounts, beating thoroughly after each addition. Pour batter into a greased 13"x9" baking pan. Bake at 350 degrees for 25 minutes, or until a toothpick tests done. Cool; cut into squares.

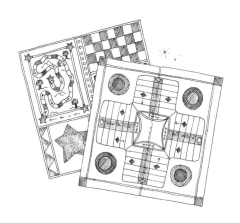

Vintage game boards make whimsical settings for game night
buffets! Check the kids' closet for forgotten games or
pick some up at yard sales. Cover with self-adhesive
clear plastic for wipe-clean ease.

Teriyaki Chicken Wings

Makes about 4 dozen

1 c. soy sauce
3/4 c. sugar
1/2 c. brown sugar, packed
1/4 c. pineapple juice
1/4 c. water

2 T. oil
1 t. garlic powder
1 t. ground ginger
4 lbs. chicken wings, separated

In a very large bowl, combine all ingredients except chicken wings; stir until sugars dissolve. Add wings; toss gently to coat. Cover and refrigerate at least 2 hours to marinate. Transfer wings to a 6-quart slow cooker. Add one cup of the marinade to slow cooker; discard remaining marinade. Cover and cook on high setting for 3-1/2 to 4-1/2 hours, until chicken juices run clear when pierced. If desired, transfer wings to a broiler pan; broil for 2 to 3 minutes, until golden.

Hollowed-out peppers make garden-fresh servers for
dips and sauces. Just cut a thin slice off the bottom
so they'll sit flat.

Tomato-Bacon Cups

Makes 2 dozen

8 slices bacon
16-oz. tube refrigerated buttermilk
   biscuits
1 ripe tomato, diced

1/2 yellow onion, diced
3/4 c. shredded Swiss cheese
1/2 c. mayonnaise

In a skillet over medium heat, cook bacon until crisp; set aside on paper towels. Meanwhile, split each biscuit horizontally into halves; press each half into a lightly greased muffin cup and set aside. In a bowl, combine crumbled bacon and remaining ingredients; mix well. Fill each biscuit with a teaspoonful of mixture. Bake at 375 degrees for 10 to 12 minutes, until golden and cheese is melted.

Good to know! If you're making hard-boiled eggs, use eggs
that have been refrigerated at least 7 to 10 days,
instead of fresher eggs...the shells will slip off easily.

Oma's Deviled Eggs

Makes one dozen

6 eggs, hard-boiled and peeled
1/4 c. mayonnaise
1 t. sweet pickle relish
1 t. sweet pickle juice, or more
   as needed

1 t. mustard
1/2 t. lemon juice
1/8 t. salt
pepper to taste
Garnish: smoked Spanish paprika

Slice eggs in half lengthwise. Remove yolks and place in a bowl; set whites on a serving platter. With a fork, mash yolks into a fine crumble. Add remaining ingredients except garnish; mix well. May add a little more pickle juice for a thinner consistency. Spoon heaping teaspoonfuls of yolk mixture into egg whites. Sprinkle with paprika; chill until serving time.

Even a simple meal of sandwiches can be memorable when it's thoughtfully served. Use the good china, set out cloth napkins and a vase of fresh flowers...after all, who's more special than family?

Farm-Fresh Spinach Quiche

Makes 8 servings

8 slices bacon, crisply cooked,
   crumbled and divided
9-inch frozen pie crust, thawed
2 c. shredded Monterey Jack cheese
10-oz. pkg. frozen chopped
   spinach, thawed and drained

1-1/2 c. milk
3 eggs, beaten
1 T. all-purpose flour

Sprinkle half of crumbled bacon in the bottom of pie crust. Mix together cheese, spinach, milk, eggs and flour; pour into crust. Sprinkle remaining crumbled bacon on top. Bake at 350 degrees for one hour, or until center is set.

Shopping for canned peaches to use in a recipe? Look for
old-fashioned canned freestone peaches...
they're closest to home-canned.

Chicken & Peaches

Makes 4 to 6 servings

1/4 c. oil
1 t. butter, melted
1 c. all-purpose flour
1/2 c. milk
2 eggs, beaten
8 bone-in chicken thighs or
   6 chicken breasts

garlic salt, salt and pepper
   to taste
15-1/4 oz. can sliced peaches in
   heavy syrup
16.3-oz. tube refrigerated flaky
   biscuits

Spread oil and melted butter in the bottom of a 3-quart casserole dish; set aside. Add flour to a shallow bowl; whisk together milk and eggs in a separate bowl. Roll chicken pieces in flour, then in egg mixture, then in flour again. Arrange chicken in casserole dish; sprinkle with seasonings. Bake, uncovered, at 400 degrees for 30 minutes, or until chicken is turning golden. Spoon peaches and syrup over chicken. Arrange biscuits in dish, pushing them down into drippings. Bake for another 12 to 15 minutes, until biscuits are golden and chicken juices run clear.

Grandma knew that cheaper cuts of beef like chuck roast and round steak are perfect for pot roast. They cook up fork-tender, juicy and flavorful...there's simply no need to purchase more expensive cuts.

Slow-Cooker Pot Roast

Makes 6 to 8 servings

3-lb. beef chuck roast

4 baking potatoes, peeled
    and quartered

6 to 8 carrots, peeled and cut
    into 2 to 3 pieces

1 onion, quartered

salt and pepper to taste

1 to 2 T. olive oil

1/4 c. butter, sliced

1.35-oz. pkg. onion soup mix

Add roast to a 6-quart slow cooker sprayed with non-stick vegetable spray. Arrange vegetables around roast. Season with salt and pepper; drizzle olive oil over all and dot vegetables with butter. Sprinkle soup mix over all. Cover and cook on low setting for for 6 to 8 hours, until roast is tender. After several hours, may spoon juices in slow cooker over vegetables once or twice.

Just-picked herbs and creamery butter...yum! Blend one cup softened butter with 2 tablespoons fresh parsley, 2 teaspoons fresh oregano and one tablespoon minced garlic. Spread over warm rolls, toss with hot noodles or dollop on steamed veggies...delicious.

Ham, Egg & Potato Supper

Makes 6 servings

1/4 c. green pepper, chopped
1/2 c. onion, chopped
2 T. butter
1 to 2 potatoes, peeled and
   thinly sliced

salt and pepper to taste
1 c. cooked ham, chopped
2 eggs, room temperature, beaten
3/4 c. shredded Cheddar cheese

In a skillet over medium heat, sauté green pepper and onion in butter for 4 minutes. Layer sliced potatoes on top; season with salt and pepper. Cook over medium-low heat for 15 minutes. Sprinkle ham over potatoes; cook another 10 minutes. Pour eggs over ham; cook another 5 to 6 minutes, until eggs are set. Sprinkle cheese on top; cover and let stand until melted.

For the flakiest biscuits, stir just enough to moisten
the flour, then gently roll or pat the dough.

Grandma's West Virginia Honey Biscuits

Makes 12 to 14 biscuits

2 c. all-purpose flour
1 T. baking powder
1/2 t. salt
1/4 c. shortening

1/4 c. honey
2/3 c. milk
1/2 t. vanilla extract

In a large bowl, combine flour, baking powder and salt; mix well. Cut in shortening with a fork until well blended; set aside. In a small bowl, mix honey, milk and vanilla. Add honey mixture gradually to flour mixture, stirring until a soft but not sticky dough is formed. Turn dough out onto a lightly floured surface; knead just enough to shape into a smooth ball. Lightly roll or pat out dough on a floured surface, 1/2-inch thick. Cut with a floured biscuit cutter; arrange biscuits on an ungreased baking sheet. Bake at 450 degrees for 12 to 15 minutes, until golden.

For hearty salads in a snap, keep cans of black olives,
garbanzo beans and marinated artichokes in the fridge.
They'll be chilled and ready to toss with fresh greens
and juicy tomatoes at a moment's notice.

Christy's Broccoli-Bacon Salad

Serves 6 to 8

1/2 lb. bacon, crisply cooked
   and chopped
1-1/2 lbs. broccoli, finely chopped

1/2 c. purple onion, sliced or diced
1 c. sweetened dried cranberries
1 c. chopped cashews or peanuts

Combine all ingredients in a large bowl. Add Dressing; mix until well coated. Cover and chill until serving time.

Dressing:

1 c. mayonnaise
1/4 c. sugar

1 T. red wine vinegar

Combine all ingredients; mix well.

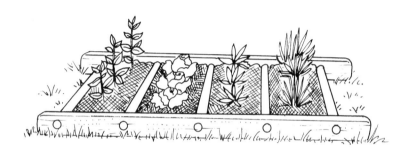

Try your hand at vegetable gardening! Even the smallest yard is sure to have a sunny corner where you can grow sun-ripened tomatoes and an herb plant or two. Seeds, plants and free advice are available at the nearest garden store.

Creamy Asparagus Bake

Serves 6 to 8

1 lb. asparagus spears, trimmed
2 T. butter
2 T. all-purpose flour
1 c. milk
1 t. lemon juice

salt to taste
3-oz. pkg. cream cheese, softened
1/2 c. soft bread crumbs
Optional: nutmeg to taste

Fill a large skillet with 3/4 inch water; bring to a boil over high heat. Add asparagus in a single layer. Cover and cook for 2 to 3 minutes, until tender; drain. Meanwhile, melt butter in a saucepan over medium heat. Blend in flour, milk, lemon juice and salt until thickened. Blend in cream cheese; remove from heat. Arrange asparagus in a buttered 2-quart casserole dish; spoon sauce over top. Sprinkle with bread crumbs. Bake, uncovered, at 350 degrees for 30 minutes. Broil for just a few minutes, until crumbs are golden. Sprinkle with nutmeg, if desired.

Keep 5 or 10 grains of rice inside your salt shaker to prevent it from clogging. A few peppercorns in your pepper shaker will do the same for your pepper and add a fresh taste too!

Gram's Dressed-Up Carrots

Makes 6 servings

16-oz. pkg. baby carrots, sliced
1/2 t. salt
1/3 c. orange marmalade
2 T. butter

2 t. Dijon mustard
1/2 t. fresh ginger, peeled
  and grated

In a saucepan, cover carrots with water; add salt and bring to a boil over high heat. Reduce heat to medium-low; cover and simmer for 10 to 12 minutes, until carrots are crisp-tender. Drain and set aside. In the same pan, combine remaining ingredients. Cook and stir over low heat until blended, about 3 minutes. Return carrots to pan; stir until glazed.

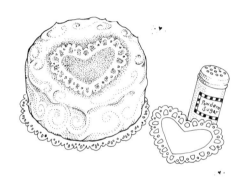

Garnish cakes and cookies in a jiffy...
sprinkle powdered sugar through a doily.

Really Fabulous Brownies

Makes 3 to 4 dozen

1 lb. butter
16-oz. pkg. semi-sweet
    chocolate chips
6-oz. pkg. unsweetened baking
    chocolate, broken
6 eggs
2 T. instant espresso coffee
    granules

2 T. vanilla extract
2-1/4 c. sugar
1-1/4 c. all-purpose flour, divided
1 T. baking powder
1 t. kosher salt
3 c. walnuts, diced
12-oz. pkg. semi-sweet
    chocolate chips

In the top of a double boiler, melt butter, larger bag of chocolate chips and baking chocolate. Cool slightly. Add eggs, one at a time; stir in coffee, vanilla and sugar. In a bowl, mix one cup flour, baking powder and salt; add to cooled chocolate mixture and set aside. In another bowl, toss walnuts and smaller bag of chocolate chips with remaining flour to coat. Add to batter and mix well. Pour batter into a greased and floured 18"x13" jelly-roll pan. Bake at 350 degrees for 15 minutes; rap pan on the countertop to eliminate any air bubbles. Bake for another 15 minutes, or until a toothpick inserted in the center comes out clean. Cool in pan; refrigerate and cut into small squares.

The best kind of friend is the kind you can sit on a porch swing with, never say a word, then walk away feeling like it was the best conversation you've ever had.

– Arnold Glasow

Luscious Angel Cupcakes

Makes 2 to 2-1/2 dozen

16-oz. pkg. angel food cake mix
3.4-oz. pkg instant vanilla pudding
   mix
2 8-oz. cans crushed pineapple

1 c. frozen whipped topping,
  thawed
2 c. assorted fresh berries

Prepare cake mix as directed on the package. Pour batter into 24 to
30 paper-lined muffin cups, filling each 2/3 full. Bake at 375 degrees for
12 to 15 minutes, until tops are golden and a toothpick tests clean. Cool
cupcakes in pan for 10 minutes; remove to wire racks to cool completely. In
a bowl, mix together dry pudding mix and undrained pineapple. Gently fold
in whipped topping; spread evenly over cupcakes. Top cupcakes with
berries; keep refrigerated until ready to serve.

Heat lemons in the microwave for 30 seconds before squeezing...you'll get twice as much juice!

Grandma's Famous Lemon Meringue Pie

Makes 8 servings

1-1/4 c. plus 6 T. sugar, divided
3 T. cornstarch
1/4 c. lemon juice
1 T. lemon zest

3 eggs, separated
1-1/2 c. boiling water
9-inch pie crust, baked and cooled

In a saucepan, combine 1-1/4 cups sugar, cornstarch, lemon juice and zest; set aside. Beat egg yolks in a small bowl and add to sugar mixture. Gradually stir in boiling water. Bring to a boil over medium heat; cook for 4 minutes, stirring constantly. Cool slightly; pour into pie crust. For meringue: in a large bowl, beat egg whites with an electric mixer on high speed until stiff peaks form. Gradually beat in remaining sugar. Spread meringue over pie filling, carefully sealing to the edges. Bake at 425 degrees for 4 to 5 minutes, until meringue is golden. Cool; cut into wedges.

Peanuts are yummy in crunchy snack mixes, but if you
need to avoid them, there are tasty substitutes to try.
Choose from raisins, sweetened dried cranberries, dried fruit
bits, candy-coated chocolates, chocolate chips and
even mini pretzel twists.

Road Trip Trail Mix

Makes about 9 cups

16-oz. pkg. dry-roasted salted
   peanuts
16-oz. pkg. salted cashews

8-oz. pkg. candy-coated chocolates
8-oz. pkg. raisins

Combine all ingredients in a large bowl; mix well. Store in an airtight container.

Dip to go! Spoon creamy vegetable dip into a tall plastic cup and add crunchy celery and carrot sticks, red pepper strips, cucumber slices and snow pea pods. Add the lid and the snack is ready to tote along. Be sure to keep it chilled.

Grilled Corn Salsa

Makes about 4 cups

6 ears sweet corn, husked
3 T. olive oil, divided
1/2 c. red onion, finely chopped
1/2 c. fresh cilantro, chopped
1 t. lemon zest

2 T. lime juice
1 t. kosher salt
2 jalapeño peppers, seeded
   and minced

Brush ears of corn with one tablespoon oil; set aside. Preheat a grill to medium-high. Grill corn, turning often, for 15 to 20 minutes, until lightly charred. Cut kernels from cobs; place in a large bowl. Add remaining oil and other ingredients; mix well. Cover and chill; keep refrigerated up to one week.

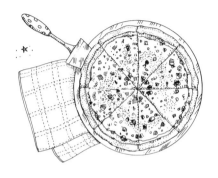

Let the kids help in the kitchen. Younger children can scrub
vegetables and tear salad greens. Older kids can measure,
chop, stir and take part in meal planning and shopping.
Give 'em a chance...they may just surprise you!

Cool Vegetable Pizza

Makes 20 servings

- 2 8-oz. tubes refrigerated crescent rolls
- 2 8-oz. pkgs. cream cheese, softened
- 1 c. mayonnaise
- 1-oz. pkg. ranch salad dressing mix
- 3/4 c. red and/or green pepper, chopped
- 3/4 c. broccoli, chopped
- 3/4 c. cauliflower, chopped
- 1/2 c. green onion, thinly sliced
- 1/2 c. tomato, chopped
- 2-oz. can sliced black olives, well drained
- 1 carrot, peeled and shredded
- 1 c. shredded Cheddar cheese

Spread both tubes of crescent dough over an ungreased 11"x7" baking sheet. Bake at 375 degrees for 10 to 12 minutes, until golden; cool completely. In a large bowl, beat cream cheese, mayonnaise and dressing mix until light and fluffy. Spread over cooled crust. Top crust with all vegetables; sprinkle cheese over all. Cover with plastic wrap; refrigerate for several hours. To serve, cut into squares.

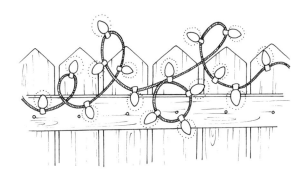

For an enchanting effect, fasten a strand of cool-burning
twinkle lights to the underside of a patio table umbrella
or along a fence.

Buffalo Chicken Wraps

Makes 8 servings

1/2 to 1 lb. bacon
1-1/2 lbs. boneless chicken
    tenderloins
1 c. buffalo wing sauce, divided
8 10-inch flour tortillas, warmed

8 lettuce leaves
1 green pepper, cut into strips
1/2 c. ranch salad dressing
Optional: additional ranch
    dressing, celery sticks

In a large skillet over medium heat, cook bacon until crisp; set aside to drain on paper towels. Meanwhile, add chicken tenderloins and 1/2 cup sauce to another skillet over medium heat. Bring to a boil; reduce heat to medium-low. Cook for 10 to 12 minutes, stirring occasionally, until chicken juices run clear when pierced. Remove chicken from heat; cool slightly, then shred with 2 forks. To serve, top each tortilla with a lettuce leaf; spoon 1/2 cup chicken mixture down the center. Top with bacon and green pepper. Drizzle with salad dressing and remaining sauce; roll up. Garnish as desired.

Try using a little less ground beef in your favorite recipe.
Add a few more chopped veggies...there's a good chance
that no one will even notice!

Angel Hair with Zucchini & Tomatoes *Makes 4 servings*

8-oz. pkg. angel hair pasta,
    uncooked
4 t. extra-virgin olive oil
4 cloves garlic, chopped
2 shallots, diced
2 zucchini, cut lengthwise into
    thin ribbons
salt and pepper to taste

3 ripe tomatoes, diced
1/4 c. low-sodium chicken or
    vegetable broth
2 T. fresh parsley, chopped
red pepper flakes to taste
Garnish: shredded Parmesan
    cheese

Cook pasta according to package directions. Drain, reserving 1/2 cup of the cooking water. Meanwhile, heat oil in a large saucepan over medium heat. Add garlic and shallots; sauté for one minute. Add zucchini and season with salt and pepper; cook for 2 minutes. Add tomatoes, broth, parsley and pepper flakes. Cook and stir for one minute; remove from heat. Add zucchini mixture to pasta and toss well, adding a little of the reserved cooking water to desired consistency. Serve with Parmesan cheese.

No peeking!
When baking, every time the oven door is opened,
the temperature drops 25 degrees.

Ripe Tomato Tart

Makes 6 servings

9-inch pie crust
1-1/2 c. shredded mozzarella
    cheese, divided
4 roma tomatoes, cut into wedges
3/4 c. fresh basil, chopped

4 cloves garlic, minced
1/2 c. mayonnaise
1/2 c. grated Parmesan cheese
1/8 t. white pepper

Line an ungreased 9" tart pan with pie crust; press crust into fluted sides of pan and trim edges. Bake at 450 degrees for 5 to 7 minutes; remove from oven. Sprinkle with 1/2 cup mozzarella cheese; let cool on a wire rack. Combine remaining ingredients; mix well and spoon into crust. Reduce heat to 375 degrees; bake for about 20 minutes, until bubbly on top.

Remember to tote along some folding stools when you go camping. There's nothing like sitting around a glowing campfire, stargazing, swapping stories and just savoring time together with family & friends!

Rebecca's Campfire Packets

Makes 4 servings

4 to 6 redskin potatoes,
   thinly sliced
1 green pepper, thinly sliced
   into strips
1 onion, sliced
2 T. olive oil

2 T. steak seasoning salt
salt and pepper to taste
Optional: 1 T. garlic, minced
4 smoked chicken sausage links,
   sliced into bite-size pieces

Spray four, 18-inch pieces of aluminum foil with non-stick vegetable spray.
Divide potatoes, pepper and onion evenly among foil pieces. Drizzle with
olive oil; sprinkle with seasonings and garlic, if using. Arrange sausage
slices on top. Wrap foil securely to form packages; place on a grill over
medium heat. Cook for 14 to 18 minutes, turning packages once, until hot
and potatoes are tender.

A child on a farm sees a plane fly overhead and dreams of a faraway place. A traveler on the plane sees the farmhouse...and dreams of home.

–Carl Burns

Summer Garden Vegetable Medley

Serves 4 to 6

1 c. potatoes, peeled and diced
1 c. yellow squash, diced
1 c. zucchini, diced
1 c. okra, sliced

1/2 c. onion, diced
salt and pepper to taste
1 c. yellow cornmeal
oil for frying

In a large bowl, mix all vegetables together. Season with salt and pepper; sprinkle with cornmeal and mix well until vegetables are coated. Heat several inches oil in a skillet over medium-high heat. Carefully add about 1-1/2 cups vegetable mixture to oil. Cook until tender and lightly golden; drain on paper towels. Repeat with remaining vegetables; serve warm.

Serve up a veggie plate for dinner...a good old Southern
tradition. With 2 or 3 scrumptious veggie dishes and
a basket of buttery cornbread, no one will miss the meat!

Confetti Corn & Rice Salad

4 ears sweet corn, husked
1-1/2 c. cooked rice
1 green pepper, halved and
   thinly sliced

1 red onion, thinly sliced
1 pt. cherry tomatoes, halved
Optional: 1 jalapeño pepper,
   thinly sliced

Boil or grill ears of corn until tender; let cool. With a sharp knife, cut corn from cob in "planks." In a serving bowl, combine rice, green pepper, red onion, tomatoes and jalapeño pepper, if using. Mix in corn, keeping some corn planks for top. Drizzle with Simple Dressing. Serve at room temperature or refrigerate overnight before serving; garnish with reserved corn planks at serving time.

Simple Dressing:

2 T. red wine vinegar
2 T. olive oil

salt and pepper to taste

Whisk all ingredients together.

You're never too old for party favors! Send your guests home with a whimsical memento...tiny potted plants, little bags of homemade candy, mini photo frames or even jars of bubble solution with wands.

Minestrone Pasta Salad

Makes 10 to 12 servings

12-oz. pkg. bow-tie pasta, uncooked

15-1/2 oz. can kidney beans, drained and rinsed

4 to 5 roma tomatoes, seeded and chopped

3-1/2 oz. pkg. sliced pepperoni

1/2 c. cubanelle or green pepper, seeded and chopped

1/4 c. fresh Italian flat-leaf parsley, chopped

1/4 c. shredded Parmesan cheese

1-1/2 t. to 1 T. fresh oregano, chopped

pepper to taste

8-oz. bottle Italian vinaigrette salad dressing

Cook pasta according to package directions; drain and rinse with cold water. In a large bowl, combine cooked pasta and remaining ingredients except salad dressing; mix well. Add desired amount of salad dressing; toss to coat. Serve immediately, or cover and refrigerate until serving time.

Take your family with you to the farmstand. Kids will
love seeing all there is to enjoy...and a taste of
juicy peach or warm tomato is a real treat!

Chilled Tomato & Fresh Basil Soup *Serves 4 to 6*

2 lbs. ripe tomatoes, cored
2 T. onion
3 T. extra-virgin olive oil
2 to 3 T. red wine vinegar or
    balsamic vinegar, divided

salt and cracked pepper to taste
1/4 c. fresh basil, finely sliced
Garnish: additional olive oil

Add tomatoes and onion to a blender; purée until smooth. If desired, strain to remove bits of tomato skin; add mixture to a large bowl. Stir in olive oil, 2 tablespoons vinegar, salt and pepper. More vinegar may be added to taste, if desired. Cover and chill for one hour or more. At serving time, ladle into bowls and top with a sprinkle of basil. Garnish with a drizzle of olive oil and serve.

Most fruit pies and desserts can be frozen up to 4 months...
a terrific way to capture the flavor of summer-ripe fruit.
Cool after baking, then wrap in plastic wrap and aluminum
foil before freezing. To serve, thaw overnight in the
fridge and warm in the oven.

Blackberry-Peach Crumble

Serves 8

2 c. fresh or frozen blackberries
2 c. sliced peaches, drained if
    canned or thawed if frozen
1 t. lemon zest
2 T. cornstarch
1 c. brown sugar, packed
    and divided

1/2 c. all-purpose flour
1/2 t. salt
Optional: 1/2 c. chopped pecans
    or almonds
1/2 c. butter
Garnish: vanilla ice cream

Combine blackberries, peaches, lemon zest, cornstarch and 1/2 cup brown sugar in a large bowl; gently mix together. Spoon fruit mixture into an 8"x8" baking pan sprayed with non-stick vegetable spray; set aside. In a separate bowl, mix together flour, salt, remaining brown sugar and nuts, if using. Cut in butter until crumbly, using 2 forks. Sprinkle crumb mixture over fruit. Bake at 375 degrees for 30 to 35 minutes, until bubbly and golden; cool for 10 to 15 minutes. Serve warm, topped with a scoop of ice cream.

Taking a cake to a potluck or get-together? Before covering
in plastic wrap, insert toothpicks into the cake and top
with mini marshmallows. They'll keep the plastic wrap
from touching the frosting.

Pineapple Sheet Cake

Makes 24 servings

2 c. all-purpose flour
2 c. sugar
2 eggs, beaten
1 c. chopped nuts, divided

2 t. baking soda
1/2 t. salt
1 t. vanilla extract
20-oz. can crushed pineapple

In a large bowl, combine flour, sugar, eggs, 3/4 cup nuts, baking soda, salt and vanilla. Add pineapple with juice and stir until well blended. Pour batter into a greased 15"x10" jelly-roll pan. Bake at 350 degrees for 20 to 22 minutes, until a toothpick inserted in the center comes out clean. Cool in pan on a wire rack. Spread cake with Icing; sprinkle with remaining nuts. Cut into squares to serve.

Icing:

8-oz. pkg. cream cheese, softened
1/2 c. butter, softened

3-1/2 c. powdered sugar
1 t. vanilla extract

In a large bowl, beat together all ingredients until smooth and spreadable.

Host a dessert party for family & friends on a
sunny afternoon. Set tables under shady trees and layer
them with quilts or checked tablecloths. Have everyone
bring their favorite dessert...sure to be fun for all!

Oatmeal Lemon Crispies

Makes 3 dozen

1 c. butter, softened
1 c. sugar
1 egg, beaten
1 t. vanilla extract

1 t. lemon extract
1-2/3 c. all-purpose flour
1/4 t. salt
1 c. old-fashioned oats, uncooked

In a large bowl, combine butter, sugar, egg and extracts. Beat with an electric mixer on medium speed. Turn mixer to low speed; slowly beat in flour and salt. Stir in oats. Drop dough by tablespoons onto parchment paper-lined baking sheets, 2 inches apart. Bake at 375 degrees for 7 to 10 minutes, until edges are lightly golden. Remove cookies to cool on wire racks. Store in a tightly covered container.

INDEX

APPETIZERS & SNACKS

Bacon-Wrapped Water Chestnuts, 37
Cheddar-Sausage Cornbread Balls, 5
Cool Vegetable Pizza, 103
Cranberry-Orange Snack Mix, 7
Grilled Corn Salsa, 101
Linda's Holiday Cranberry Salsa, 39
Oma's Deviled Eggs, 75
Road Trip Trail Mix, 99
Roasted Red Pepper &
    Artichoke Dip, 3
Teriyaki Chicken Wings, 71
Tomato-Bacon Cups, 73
Traditional Christmas Hot
    Crab Dip, 41

BREADS

Butterball Biscuits, 19
Crazy-Good Popovers, 53
Grandma's West Virginia Honey
    Biscuits, 85

DESSERTS

Blackberry-Peach Crumble, 121
Caramel Apple Cupcakes, 31
Christmas Peppermint Cookies, 67
Grandma's Famous Lemon
    Meringue Pie, 97
Grandma's Gingerbread Cake, 69
Luscious Angel Cupcakes, 95
Oatmeal Lemon Crispies, 125
Pineapple Sheet Cake, 123
Really Fabulous Brownies, 93
Spiderweb Cookies, 35
Strawberries in the Snow, 65
Warm Banana Bread Cobbler, 33

MAINS

Angel Hair with Zucchini &
    Tomatoes, 107
Bake-All-Day Barbecue Beef, 17
Baked Macaroni My Way, 47
Buffalo Chicken Wraps, 105

INDEX

Chicken & Peaches, 79
Elegant Beef & Noodles, 43
Farm-Fresh Spinach Quiche, 77
Ham, Egg & Potato Supper, 83
Herbed Turkey Breast, 13
One-Pot Pork Chop Dinner, 45
Rebecca's Campfire Packets, 111
Ripe Tomato Tart, 109
Scalloped Potatoes & Ham, 49
Shrimp Fettuccine Alfredo, 51
Slow-Cooker Pot Roast, 81
Turkey Enchilada Skillet, 15
Upside-Down Pizza, 9
Zucchini & Sausage Casserole, 11

SALADS

Christy's Broccoli-Bacon Salad, 87
Confetti Corn & Rice Salad, 115
Cranberry Pretzel Salad, 25
Minestrone Pasta Salad, 117
Winter Garden Salad, 55

SIDES

Best Cheesy Potatoes, 23
Creamy Asparagus Bake, 89
Gram's Dressed-Up Carrots, 91
Mom's Cheesy Broccoli Bake, 59
Pumpkin Pie Applesauce, 21
Summer Garden Vegetable
    Medley, 113
Sweet Potato Crisp, 57

SOUPS

Chilled Tomato & Fresh
    Basil Soup, 119
Easy Italian Wedding Soup, 61
Farmstand Vegetable Soup, 27
October Bisque, 29
Snowy-Day Stew, 63

Our Story

Back in 1984, we were next-door neighbors raising our families in the little town of Delaware, Ohio. Two moms with small children, we were looking for a way to do what we loved and stay home with the kids too. We had always shared a love of home cooking and making memories with family & friends and so, after many a conversation over the backyard fence, **Gooseberry Patch** was born.

We put together our first catalog at our kitchen tables, enlisting the help of our loved ones wherever we could. From that very first mailing, we found an immediate connection with many of our customers and it wasn't long before we began receiving letters, photos and recipes from these new friends. In 1992, we put together our very first cookbook, compiled from hundreds of these recipes and, the rest, as they say, is history.

Hard to believe it's been almost 40 years since those kitchen-table days! From that original little **Gooseberry Patch** family, we've grown to include an amazing group of creative folks who love cooking, decorating and creating as much as we do. Today, we're best known for our homestyle, family-friendly cookbooks, now recognized as national bestsellers.

One thing's for sure, we couldn't have done it without our friends all across the country. Each year, we're honored to turn thousands of your recipes into our collectible cookbooks. Our hope is that each book captures the stories and heart of all of you who have shared with us. Whether you've been with us since the beginning or are just discovering us, welcome to the **Gooseberry Patch** family!

Jo Ann & Vickie

Visit our website anytime
www.gooseberrypatch.com

Email

1·800·854·6673